Homing in the Presence
Meditations for Daily Living

Homing in the Presence
Meditations for Daily Living

by Gerhard E. Frost

Illustrated by Gemma Rossini Cullen

Winston Press

Acknowledgements

Book design by Maria Mazzara · Schade
All biblical quotations, unless otherwise
indicated, are from the *Revised Standard Version of the Bible,*
copyrighted 1946, 1952, © 1971, 1973.

ISBN: 0-86683-756-6 (previously ISBN: 0-03-043921-3)

Winston Press, 430 Oak Grove
Minneapolis, Minnesota 55403

5 4 3

Printed in the United States of America.

Contents

Beginning Our Journey:
An Introduction

One dark evening in mid-November, I was waiting for a bus in Teaneck, New Jersey, when I was startled by what sounded like the honking of wild geese. It can't be so, I thought. I must have brought it with me, this Minnesota sound. And so I dismissed the thought as I boarded the bus.

The next morning at the same intersection, I heard the sound again. This time, though, I could see! I hadn't been imagining things after all. Wistfully, I watched the fluid beauty of those magnificent V's until they were out of sight. Then I turned to face another day.

All during that day, I felt as if I'd been visited by deep meaning. Those geese, I thought, go back a long way. Before there was a Boston, or a New York City, or a Baltimore, the wild geese were making their way down the Eastern seaboard. For centuries, they've responded to the call of the seasons as they've homed in God's world. Their journeys, their repeated homings, are suggestive for me.

Homing. Home. Home means habit, a pattern of thinking and imagining, of wanting and enjoying. Home is where I live in gracious repetition and invitation. I turn the same doorknob. I hear the same voices. I look into the same eyes and see love and acceptance there. True, these habits bring with them a host of duties and responsibilities — but duty seems too tame a word for love.

As I think about those geese, I'm filled with a sense of belonging. I know that God is my home. I feel my own solidarity with those who've lived and believed before me. I reach across the centuries as I affirm with them, "Lord, thou hast been our dwelling place in all generations. Before the mountains were brought forth, or ever thou hadst formed the earth and the world, from everlasting to everlasting thou art God." He always has been, and always will be. That's the way I want it!

This book invites you to reflect on the inward journey. It is the longest journey of all, the journey home. It is a journey toward knowing God and being known by him. It is, itself, a sharing and a homing in the everlasting mercy. So, come with me.

Chapter One:

Homing in Hope

Lord, thou hast been our dwelling place
in all generations.
Before the mountains were brought forth,
or ever thou hadst formed the earth
and the world, from everlasting
to everlasting thou art God.

Psalm 90:1-2

I'm Restless, Lord

This afternoon I saw them,
hundreds of snow geese,
and I'm caught in the spell
of another, more wonderful world.

As I travelled a country road in Texas,
there they were in the rice fields.
And above them
a few on the wing, "just testing,"
I'm sure, testing their wings
for The Day.

How can they know, I wondered.
What makes them rise up together
and fill the sky?
Who signals The Moment?
Are they caught
in some nameless restlessness
as The Time draws near?
Who gives the sign?
And which of them knows
when to slice the wind
at the tip of the V,
when to begin The Journey?

One day they'll pass me by,
fly high in my Minnesota sky
on their way into northern blue.

I'm restless, Lord,
restless "until my heart
finds rest in You."

And yet, I keep telling myself,
as I hear home sounds,
that I'm not old—
just sixty-nine, I say.

But I say it often now.
It just won't stay said.

Homing in Hope

May the God of hope fill you with all joy and peace in believing, so that by the power of the Holy Spirit you may abound in hope.

Romans 15:13

Observe the traffic of children if you would know the meaning of home and hope. In every mood they turn toward home. Whatever their need of the moment, they are great homers.

Sometimes with a tear on each cheek; sometimes with a secret too good to keep; sometimes with a question that won't wait; sometimes just hungry, or tired, or guilty — always the child turns toward home. The unlocked door is the child's symbol of hope.

As members in the body of Christ, we home in the Everlasting. Sometimes we come for comfort from the rubble of our broken dreams; sometimes to cup our thirsty why's up to the wisdom and love of God — always we come to hear our names, to be held and cherished and loved.

Our lives are meant to be shaped by our faith, or, rather, by the object of our faith. Our goals are intended to be set in the context of Gift — God's gift of hope which gives us strength and sustenance. However far our personal goals take us, we still need to return to our home, to our Father, for the hope that makes our wandering possible.

Not in Our Handwriting

The seventy returned with joy, saying, "Lord, even the demons are subject to us in your name!" And he said to them . . . "Do not rejoice in this, that the spirits are subject to you; but rejoice that your names are written in heaven."

Luke 10:17-20

Some years ago, a reporter was interviewing a famous athlete about his long and successful career in baseball. Toward the end of the interview, the reporter asked, "What was the biggest thrill of your entire career?"

The athlete surprised his questioner by answering, "Every time I put on my suit."

It was a great answer. It suggests that people aren't sustained so much by single moments as they are by the steadying fact of belonging. The moments of glory may be exciting, but deeper personal satisfaction comes from being a part of something lasting and whole.

Jesus sent the seventy ahead of him to preach and to heal. When they came home, it must have been great fun to have so much show-and-tell, so much bring-and-brag—an exciting time for all. Success is pleasant whenever it comes and it's natural to enjoy it. But Jesus is warning them about misplaced priorities: *Do not rejoice in this.* In all your activity and planning, he says, don't depend on statistics and measurable results, for they may not last. Instead, let your joy rest first in your acceptance by me and the fact that I count you in. You belong to me. Who and whose you are—these are the important facts. *Your names are written in heaven.*

In the process of living, we have left trails of signatures behind us—at weddings and funerals, in all kinds of social and business transactions. But there is a heavenly transaction, an awesome arrangement of inheritance, where both God's name and ours are written in his authoritative hand. In every place and under every condition we have this abundant reason for joy: Our names are written in heaven, not as signatures in our handwriting, but as family records in the Father's hand.

I'm Not Lost

As Christians, we home in God the Father. We know that he has found us, and we return to him again and again—in sorrow, in joy, in praise. We walk through the unlocked door and call his name. We go to him in prayer. He is always there.

Dr. Helmut Thielicke has observed, "God is always there first, and therefore our praying is always only an answer to this simple fact." We don't strike up the conversation with God. His is the first word—and that word is his only Son; *the Word was with God, and the Word was God.*

God's word provides us with an unfailing sense of direction. As long as we listen, and learn, and respond, we always know where we are.

There was once a powerful man, important in the world of business. He was accustomed to command, to having his own way. One day, late for an appointment, he decided to take a shortcut. To his dismay, he soon found that he'd chosen the wrong road. He realized he was completely lost, and determined to ask the first person he saw for directions.

That person was a child. He addressed the young boy gruffly, "Boy, which way to Dover?"

"I don't know," the child responded, embarrassed.

"Well then," the man demanded, "how far to Paynesville?"

"I don't know that either," the child answered.

The man's questions got angrier as the boy kept responding with the same answer. The boy grew more and more uncomfortable and, finally, the man lost his temper and shouted, "You don't know much, do you?"

Then, for the first time, the boy smiled. Looking up the winding road to a little house where the evening light shone through the window, the boy exclaimed, "No, but I ain't *lost*."

No matter how powerful we are, our power means nothing if we're lost. Our true power comes from believing in God's presence as the first Word. With this belief, we never lose sight of our home. To trust in God, even when we're facing the unknown, is to proclaim to all the world, "I'm not lost."

Taking the Home Road

As far back as she can remember, our granddaughter has loved her overnights with Grandma and Granddaddy. It's become a ritual of sorts: we drive to her house, she welcomes us with a hug, and we carry her overnight bag out to the car. She chatters all the way to our house, waiting eagerly for each familiar street and landmark along the way.

Recently I took a different road, one that was unfamiliar to her, and she was disappointed. "Next time, don't do that!" she said reprovingly.

This instance was one of many in which I've learned a lesson from a child. A familiar road, a road we travel by habit, isn't an old road at all. Memory and expectation keep it always new. This is the secret our granddaughter taught me that day: Repetition isn't always repetitious. It can be welcomed and cherished.

When I go home, I expect a familiar experience with familiar people. I turn into the same driveway, open the same door, hear the same voices, sit at the same table, and share bread with the same people. I receive the same message, spoken or unspoken, but expressed in countless ways. And I expect to respond. I want to keep up-to-date in my important relationships.

Home is, indeed, a place of continual repetition through which love, like nature itself, finds the power to stay new. This morning's sunshine, air, and water are new, and I receive their freshness with joy. I celebrate the goodness of God in the self-replenishing gift of his love.

As we travel the familiar road with God, we too recognize familiar landmarks. We pray well-known prayers and participate in familiar rituals to keep ourselves up-to-date with God, for although he never falls behind, we sometimes do. The benediction I receive today isn't the same as yesterday because my history of grace has lengthened. My capacity to receive has increased. Our Lord's Prayer, when I pray it today, isn't the same as yesterday, for I am different.

Clifton Fadiman once said that when we reread a classic we don't see more in the book than we did before, we see more in *ourselves*.

God's eternal love is ever new. As we take the familiar road home, we are — like nature's gifts — renewed.

Do Not Erase

I carry a picture in my mind of the world-famous mathematician and physicist, Dr. Albert Einstein. For almost a year, he lived on our street in the little New

Jersey town of Princeton. I remember seeing him as he walked to and from his work at the Institute of Scientific Research, the long hair flowing, the sensitive face — an extraordinary man.

Many stories have been told about him over the years, and one remains my special favorite. On a Friday afternoon, the story goes, a cleaning person arrived at the Institute to prepare the classrooms for the next week. When she came to Dr. Einstein's seminar room, she found, as one might expect, that sections of the blackboard were covered with intricate equations and formulas. Over these, Dr. Einstein had boldly scrawled, *Erase*.

There was one section, however, over which he had carefully written *Do not erase*. And below it was only this: *2 + 2 = 4*.

I have often wondered what Dr. Einstein was trying to say with those instructions. Was he telling his students — and us — that the mind can wander far if it knows its home? Was he reminding himself of that fact? True, it's often easier to deal with the complexities of life if we keep reminding ourselves of its simplicities. Perhaps this was Dr. Einstein's message.

Someone has whimsically said that there's no subject, however complex, which — if we study with patience and intelligence — we can't make more complex. We'll never conquer the horizons of the unknown.

While it's a mistake to oversimplify the complex, it can be even more of a mistake to overcomplicate the simple. As we apply this principle to our life of faith, we need to remember that our overcomplicating can hide the basic facts of God's acceptance of us and our belonging to him.

The process of real learning makes it abundantly clear that the more we know about something, the more we're conscious of what we *don't* know. We will never know it all, but we can keep returning to the essential facts of God's faithfulness and his power to save.

Our salvation is God's gift to us. This is our home and our comfort. And, in the midst of our complicated lives, this is the one truth over which we should write *Do not erase.*

Let God Be God

Look at the birds of the air: they neither sow nor reap nor gather into barns, and yet your heavenly Father feeds them. Are you not of more value than they? ...Consider the lilies of the field, how they grow; they neither toil nor spin; yet I tell you, even Solomon in all his glory was not arrayed like one of these.

Matthew 6:26−29

Perhaps I speak for you, too, when I confess that I tend to waste my energies in regretting the past and worrying about the future. I've lost many a present moment in this self-defeating process. Even though I know that there's only one who can cover the past with forgiveness and light the future with promise—and I know that his name is God—I often forget to *let him be* God. I forget what I've always known: that God takes care of his creatures.

When Jesus draws our attention to the birds and the lilies, he seems to be saying, "Be at peace with God's plan for you. Do only what you're equipped to do, and let God take care of the rest." The birds don't worry about things they can't do—like

sowing and reaping. And the lilies
aren't bothered by the fact that they
can't toil or spin. God feeds them and
clothes them, and frees them to do what they
do best: the birds to sing, the lilies to grow
in beauty and fragrance.

My distrust of God is my great
burden. He knows this, and so he invites me
to rest in his promise, to accept my
humanity and rejoice in my dependence on
him. He offers me this golden key to each
new day: Let God be God.

Anita and Lee

*Lord, thou hast been our dwelling place
in all generations.*

Psalm 90:1

Anita and her husband, Lee, live in
the silent vastness of Navajoland
amid the wind-sculpted Arizona desert. They
have raised seven sons, all of whom are
grown and make their lives elsewhere. Now
Anita and Lee are alone.

When we visited them, we found Anita tending her sheep and goats on the rim of the canyon, a short distance from her hogan. She spied our Land Rover as soon as we approached, for she was expecting us. She seemed to carry herself effortlessly over the difficult terrain as she hurried to welcome us. Later, we gathered in the one-room hogan — our interpreter, the pastor, four girls from the mission school, my wife, and I. Together with our hostess, we formed a close circle.

After a brief conversation, I asked, "Where's Lee?"

"He'll be here soon," Anita replied. "He's breaking a horse."

I went outside, and there he was, not far away, skillfully maneuvering his sweaty, unruly mount as it circled, stopped, and started on its reluctant journey home.

When Lee arrived, we made room for him in our circle of talk and prayer. We had brought some Navajo hymn books, and we each chose a favorite. When Anita's turn came, she selected "This World Is Not My Home."

I wondered about that as we sang. After years of living in the same place, of raising seven sons, of tending her animals daily, she had chosen that song. Surrounded by the beauty of the Arizona desert, committed to an active and varied routine, she still knew that her home was in the Lord.

This world is but a bridge; pass over it, but build no house upon it. I've thought about this old saying, too. Is this what it is to walk by faith—to live by grace? We can love this visible world as God loves it, but still remember that it isn't our home. We can explore and enjoy this world's wonders, but not confuse means with ends. We need not make a home of what God intends to be a bridge.

Unusual people, Anita and Lee, memorable to me for their grace of speech and manner, for their energetic beauty at ages sixty-three and sixty-eight, but most of all for their serene and tempered wisdom.

Chapter Two:

Knowing the Father

Your Father knows what you need before you ask him. Pray then like this: Our Father who art in heaven . . . .

Matthew 6:8-9

My Soul Waits

There must be dry times;
all living things must wait
and be tested.
All things that grow
share one secret,
the mystery of hidden pain.

The grain of wheat
must suffer early season dryness,
those miniature droughts,
not too long, but real.
They make for depth
through struggle.

Young roots must *reach*
lest shallow-rooted greenness
prove insufficient to the harvest.

I, too, struggle
to reach deeper.
I'm afraid, Lord, afraid
of being too much surface
with insufficient depth.
I suffer the dry times.
My soul awaits the rain.

The secret of the wheat field
is my secret, too.

Be Good to Yourself

For if our hearts condemn us, God is greater than our hearts and knoweth all things.
                    1 John 3:20, King James Version

Does your mind wander when you try to center your thoughts on God? Does it race ahead one moment and lag behind the next? Do you find that your heart is wild and untamed whenever you try to pray? When you can't seem to control your thoughts, do you rise up in frustration and self-directed anger?

Consider these words of St. Francis de Sales: "When your heart is wandering or distracted, bring it back quietly to its point, restore it tenderly to its Master's side; and if you did nothing else the whole of your hour but bring back your heart patiently and put it near our Lord again, and every time you put it back again it turned away again, your hour would be well employed."

Notice the words *quietly, tenderly, patiently.* Think about them for a moment. Sometimes your thoughts and your heart will behave like unruly children. They'll want to go their own way. How will you answer them — by scolding yourself? Again, remember the words: *quietly, tenderly, patiently.*

Self-discipline can easily turn into self-hatred. At times like these, when we simply *can't* pray or center our thoughts on God, we need to remind ourselves that God is patient and kind. He takes no pleasure in our guilt or self-inflicted misery. Instead, he comes to us, reaches for us, and rescues us from ourselves. He looks for us — and finds us — even when our hearts and minds wander. He is familiar with the wilderness and wasteland we create for ourselves, and he leads us across it to safety. *If your heart condemns you, God is greater than your heart and knows all things.*

Looking Forward

By faith he sojourned in the land of promise, as in a foreign land, living in tents . . . . For he looked forward to the city which has foundations, whose builder and maker is God.

Hebrews 11:9-10

During a recent interview, the actor Yul Brynner revealed that he comes from a long line of Gypsies on his mother's side. When he was asked why Gypsies are always on the move, he replied that travel is an important part of their religion. They believe in the newness of each day, and they celebrate this newness by living as roving nomads, going from place to place in strange lands. They believe that settling down and becoming too attached to any bit of this world would violate their faith.

This concept isn't alien to the Christian faith. Like Abraham, we face into a promise each day. Our creeds leave us looking forward and upward.

While we aren't called to ignore this present world or to be indifferent to its problems, we are asked to travel light. Letting ourselves get lost in daily problems is a violation of *our* faith. We too are gypsies and backpackers; God asks us to carry our home and our hope wherever we go.

Praying the Names

Our help is in the name of the Lord, who made heaven and earth.
Psalm 124:8

God has created a world in which form suits function. If you examine the skeletal structure of a bird, you can see that it is intended to fly. If you do the same with a fish, you can tell that it lives in the water. But humanity doesn't yield its secret so readily. Human beings have special purposes that are not revealed by studying our form alone. We are created in God's image. We are meant to include God in our total response to living.

God has added to us a special dimension, the ability to worship and to pray. We can do what no other living things can do: We can call on God by name.

God has many names which help express his nature and purpose, his essence and his will. No single name can adequately describe him, for he is more than a father, more than a creator, more than a ruler. All of them together are a human effort to express the inexpressible glory, majesty, and humanity of God's being.

More than just describing God, his names can be our simplest prayers to him. Infants, unable to verbalize what they need, simply cry out *Mommy* and *Daddy*. Like infants, we need only cry out God's name—this special way to pray—and our helplessness finds comfort.

Indeed, *our help is in the name of the Lord.*

When You Can't Pray

I t's often when I most need to pray that I'm least able. Sometimes I'm too crushed and dispirited; at other times, I'm too confused and panic-stricken. I find it impossible to marshal my thoughts or command the right words. A flood of feeling drowns all coherence, and I can't talk with God in an orderly way.

Does this sound familiar to you? Let me share something with you that's worked for me at times like these.

When my inner self is in chaos and I'm simply unable to pray, no matter how much I want or need to, I find comfort in recalling and speaking the many biblical names of God. I say them slowly, one at a time, allowing myself to experience him, asking myself what each name means to me. I try to settle back with each name, sinking my whole weight into it and breathing deeply in faith. I don't make any attempt to explain anything to myself or to God. Rather, I let him speak to me through his names.

God. Maker. Ruler. Eternal One. Father. Lover of the World.

Jesus. Lord. Christ. Savior. Redeemer. Messiah. Emmanuel. Son of God. Son of Man. Prince of Peace. Good Shepherd. Bread of Life. Light of the World. Living Water. The Way. The Truth. The Life. Lord of Lords. King of Kings. God's "Yes." Master. Teacher. Friend.

Holy Spirit. Comforter. Spirit of Truth.
Spirit of Christ. Creator Spirit. Life-giving Spirit.

These are only some of God's names, and each one is a gift of himself to me. In them, I meet him, and he makes himself known.

Then I mingle the names of people I love with these names of God. I mention those who are in special need, naming them before God, simply bringing them to him and leaving them there. I rest in the understanding that God doesn't need my opinion about any of them. He doesn't even need me to tell him why I'm saying their names. I know that he knows why.

God asks only that I call upon him. His answer awaits my call.

Louder Than Words

Not long ago, some friends and I were talking about times when our prayers carry us beyond words. Sometimes, we all admitted, our feelings of grief or joy are so strong that we're left speechless before God.

One friend remarked, "It was a great experience for me to discover, after trying in vain to express my needs in orderly thoughts, that I could be healed and blessed by my Father by *just sitting* with him!"

The remark reminded me of treasured times in my own life, when I was living with my growing-up but not yet grown-up children. Often, before bedtime, one or another of them would come to me and say, "May I sit with you, Dad?" Then, without embarrassment to either of us, a long-limbed fledgling would settle into my lap. I remember best the moments when we *just sat* for a while, without speaking, enjoying each other in the sacrament of silence.

I won't forget the warmth and affection of those times. Both the child and I did some growing then. We felt mutual joy, but even more important was the inner nourishment we gained and the way our relationship was strengthened. The effects of those moments have never lessened with the passing years.

Today, as we "sit with our Father," we may be filled with joys and sorrows which leave us without words, but never without his caring compassion. We don't need to try to avoid the stillness, or fear our own speechlessness, for sympathetic, loving silence is one of the choicest fruits of any relationship. It can speak louder than words.

Asking the Father

When we cry Abba! Father! it is the Spirit himself bearing witness with our spirit that we are children of God, and if children, then heirs, heirs of God and fellow heirs with Christ, provided we suffer with him in order that we may also be glorified with him.

Romans 8:15-17

God gives me the right, through his grace, to call him *Father.* This family name was made meaningful by Christ, and becomes real to us through the inspiration of the Holy Spirit. When we experience God as *Our Father,* we know the Spirit's work has surely taken root in us.

This being true, our Lord's Prayer isn't simply a prayer we recite in haste. Perfect in form and content, it is the permanent base for every conversation with God.

In our Lord's Prayer, God teaches me to attack my unbelief and timidity by making bold claims. Since God is my Father, I needn't limit myself by small vision and petty requests. I believe the words Jesus said: "It is your Father's good pleasure to give you the kingdom." With the extravagant faith of a child, I open myself to his best gifts and honor him with my large expectations.

As his child, I ask with assurance, knowing that even the painful answers still lead to the enduring blessing of the Father, whose kingdom is one of righteousness, peace, and joy.

A Family Prayer

When the disciples asked "Lord, teach us to pray," Jesus gave them the Lord's Prayer. So it is itself an answer to a prayer, perfect in content and form. The prayer is more than a list of petitions, from us to God; it is like a beating heart, with the back and forth movement of God's coming to us and our responding to him.

The opening words tell us much about the fellowship and love of Christian discipleship. The first word, *Our,* warmed by the comforting image of *Father,* stresses our family relationship to God and to each other. I need you, and you need me, and we both need God. I mustn't elbow you away or insist on being the only child; we must learn to live and work together. God's gifts are enough for all of his children. We can't be strangers to each other if we invoke the same Father.

Sometimes we hear people say that blood is thicker than water. But faith is even thicker than blood. I'm closer to someone who shares my faith, although not blood-related, than I am to a blood-relative who doesn't.

The word *our* suggests folded hands—not my own hands clasping each other, but our hands clasped together. Joined hands speak truly of our Father. We cut ourselves off from the power of the Holy Spirit whenever we forget or neglect our fellowship in Christ. As an arm can serve the body only when it's connected to that body, a person is free to serve others only when he or she is bound to them in love.

Our Lord's Prayer is a family prayer, and it spans the whole world. When we say *who art in heaven,* we aren't locating God in terms of place but identifying his limitless grace. This prayer knows no divisions and respects no barriers. Through it, we are all brothers and sisters. As Jesus said, "My mother and my brothers are those who hear the word of God and do it." By praying this prayer and shaping our lives around it, we find a place for ourselves in God's loving family.

God Is for Me

As I write these lines a man is raising the flag on the school ground across the street. I watch him, and think of the prayer words *Thy will be done.* I think of how often I've prayed those words and ducked, preparing for the worst instead of expecting the best. It's as if God is my adversary instead of my friend. I have been suspicious of him, forgetting that "If God is for us, who is against us? He who did not spare his own Son but gave him up for us all, will he not also give us all things with him?''

God is, indeed, for me. This prayer calls for a glad flag-raising in my soul; instead I have flown it at half-mast. My mood has too often been one of submission and joyless resignation.

God's will for us isn't only best, it is the only good. Not a sigh, then, but a song, befits our praying of *Thy will be done.* This prayer commits me to God's work. In it, I stand up and am counted. Through it, I volunteer to further his purpose, to do more than wait idly for others to serve and obey. This prayer is my pledge to Christian action.

With Good Grace

With good grace was a common expression in our home as I was growing up. But I wasn't sure of its meaning.

At first I thought the phrase meant that you smiled—even if you had to fake it—when choicest play was interrupted by some errand or household chore.

Then, gradually, I learned that it was
a certain way of doing things. "If you won't
do it with good grace, don't do it at all,"
my mother sometimes said.

I recall my eventual repentance, to
which she responded, "You were unwilling,
so I've done it myself." This was punishment
indeed, to be denied a second chance by seeing
my *won't* become *can't*.

Today our Lord says *Go . . . Visit
. . . Feed . . . Clothe,* and he seems to add
with good grace. I know now what he means.
Do it with a flair, with a little hop-skip-and-
jump, with some heavenly class! Our Father
gives us this day, but not forever, to do his
will on earth. We commit ourselves to joy in
service when we pray *Thy will be done on earth
as it is in heaven.*

Grace is the gift of undeserved
goodness in the form of forgiveness. It is
God reaching down to us, the unworthy, the
sinful, the little ones. This forgiveness, once
received, becomes new energy for a new
task, done in God's way.

Long Distance

We were talking across the continent on the telephone, our daughter, her mother, and I. The conversation hadn't depressed us, but the import of the discussion weighed upon us, and now we hesitated to say good-bye.

I can't explain what I did then, for we aren't a spiritually demonstrative family, given to pious gimmicks. On some surprising impulse, I found myself saying, "Before we hang up, let's pray the *Our Father*." So we did, and then we said good-night.

I've been thinking about that phone call. What strange opportunities lie hidden in our mechanical inventions. Perhaps we can make more personal and spiritual use of the technology that surrounds us and remember that our machines can be our servants. In our day, when we experience so many kinds of distance, I have heard loneliness described as the mass neurosis of our time. When *long distance* is first a matter of the heart and mind, perhaps we can find no better way of bridging the gaps between us than in the prayer of communion, our family prayer. In early Christian times, when long distance was spanned by message bearers, many New Testament greetings suggest the "ourness" of Christian fellowship. Can we recapture this spirit for our age of hurried and harried people?

Chapter Three:

This Is the Day

This is the day which the Lord has made;
let us rejoice and be glad in it.

Psalm 118:24

The Tree

Today I plant a tree,
a tiny seedling,
as I say:

I place you here
for faces I will never see.

Grow tall,
reach for the sky,
stretch toward the sun.
All moments meet in you,
all seasons that have
ever been.

Grow tall,
that, as I now
look down in tenderness,
those faces will
look up in awe.

Speak.
Tell your story
of manger, yoke, and cross,
the story of
the Tree.

This Is the Day

This is the day which the Lord has made;
let us rejoice and be glad in it.

Psalm 118:24

It was an international seminar on religion. There were thirteen in the class, each from a different country, and I was the teacher. We didn't speak the same language or come from the same background or culture, but we were members of the same family — the family of "Our Father."

One morning, as the class was about to begin and the members were finding their places, I asked on impulse, "What keeps you going?" After a moment of reflection the man from Ghana answered, "I believe God wants me to be." That was all he said, and it made my day.

Not one of us asked to be born. None of us really understands this mystery of the gift of life — not the wisest scientist, or the most knowledgeable philosopher – and none of us earned it. God has simply given it, as he has given so many other things. We search for good news and we have it: God is our creator. He has loved us into existence, and his love keeps us going.

God wants us to be. This truth is new every moment of our lives. The God with whom we live in all eternity is our Father today. Because of this, we have a reason for living — not in yesterday, or in tomorrow, but in *today*.

While we need to look ahead, we must never look past the present. *Now* is God's moment, and his meeting place with us. It is alive with his presence and laden with his love. This day is a bringer of gifts.

A Child of Light

. . . *once you were darkness, but now you are light in the Lord; walk as children of light . . . and try to learn what is pleasing to the Lord.*

Ephesians 5:8, 10

God wants me to be, and he wants me to be more than I am. He wants me to know him and his intentions for me. He invites me to know myself by looking to him, for he alone is the way to true self-knowledge. All that I am is shown in my response to Jesus Christ, in the wonder I feel as I love and serve him.

I know all this to be true and yet sometimes I forget. I seem to wish I were a simpler creature. At these times, I envy the limited appetites and aspirations of the animal, as though it, rather than Christ, represents my lost paradise.

The materialist lives within me. I can see it as I shrink from life's hard questions and try to confine myself to the finite satisfactions of eating, sleeping, arranging my household. These activities can keep me submerged in the shallows of life, lost in

unbelief, dreamlessness, a willingness to
settle for so little.

But Jesus said, "I came that they
may have life, and have it abundantly."
Why can't I remember that? It may be that
God's high purpose frightens me. His truth
claims me, carries me into situations I would
like to avoid. I pull back from the dangerous
freedoms and opportunities he puts before
me. Yet still I remember Jesus reminded us
that we "shall not live by bread alone, but
by every word that proceeds from the
mouth of God."

My struggle goes on. I know that on
this very day abundance awaits me to the
degree that I am open to his gifts and
guidance, to the degree that I can trust in
his love and take the risks of faith.

Morning by Morning

Morning by morning they gathered it, each as much as he could eat; but when the sun grew hot, it melted.

Exodus 16:21

It seemed like such a strange and wasteful arrangement! God had commanded his people to gather only as much manna as they could eat in a single day — no more, and no less. Every morning, the ground was covered with it, like frost; anyone who tried to keep some overnight woke up to find it spoiled.

Why weren't the people allowed to store the manna? Why didn't God give them a six-months' supply at a time? What was he saying to them by this daily generosity?

The manna was more than food. It served as a reminder of God's promise, a sign of his faithfulness. God knew that if the people could stockpile it, they'd take his goodness for granted and forget who was caring for them. So it had to be a hand-to-mouth arrangement. Fresh manna would express God's ever-new love. New food would mean new growth in the grace of his relationship with his people.

Today, with cupboards, refrigerators, and freezers, we may forget that God's goodness is moment by moment, morning by morning. He gives us help in pace with our need — no more, no less. His love is as alive as blood and breath. We live by one pulse of blood and two lungs full of breath at a time. Our spirits live on the momentary movements of God's great mercy.

"It took me so long to learn the lesson of *this day* when I prayed," an aged friend once told me. This is one of life's most difficult lessons, and one of the last to be learned. Each new moment tells us that we're remembered by the one who created it and us. It's both his signature and his gift.

Today isn't a warmed-over yesterday; the present isn't a left-over past. As we walk by faith, we see the Christ-face of the future welcoming us.

God the Father gives us each new day, like manna, morning by morning.

Proud Moments

We had decided to take our four-year-old granddaughter on her first overnight in our North Woods cabin. When bedtime came, we tucked her in with much care and some misgivings, for it was very cold that night.

Hours later, I awoke to sounds of uncomfortable restlessness coming from her bed. "She's cold," I thought. "She must have kicked the blankets off."

I went to her bed and, of course, she had. Instead of merely covering her again, I joined her, promising that I'd stay with her through the night. I tucked the blankets around us both and held her small cold feet in my hands.

After a bit of cozying and conversation, she turned her curly head toward the wall. Then, just as I thought she was falling asleep, she turned to me and said, "I like the way you talk."

A proud moment! I can live for a long time on that.

There is another memory — this one from the shadow side of my experience — of my aged mother one week before she died. I'd spent the night with her, then "walked" with her through the worship service in her hymnal, for it was Sunday morning.

Words came hard for her. As I helped her with her breakfast, I sensed that she was distracted. "Is there something you want to tell me?" I asked.

With great difficulty, the words came. "You've made a good day."

Another of my proudest moments.

These two memories stay with me. Honors come to all of us; some tarnish, and some fade away. The stuff of life is made of personal relationships, the repeated and common experiences of *this day*. The trust of a child, the gratitude and affection of an aged person—these are among the lasting honors we return to again and again.

Boasting of these moments doesn't embarrass me; we all have such things to cherish, and moments like these come to us almost casually as we live with one another in the dailiness of human love and responsibility. Our Father is too impartial to hang the choicest honors high. He provides us, his children, with daily situations which contain within them the highest and the best.

Behold, the Lamb

*. . . and he looked at Jesus as he walked, and said,
"Behold, the Lamb of God!"*

John 1:36

I was teaching a confirmation class
of sixteen young Navajo Christians,
and we were discussing the subject of time as
God's gift of opportunity. We talked about
our own mortality, and then discussed why
we measure time. I stepped to the
blackboard and wrote *May 2, 1977 A.D.*

I stood there for a few moments as
we considered how we have divided the
centuries into *B.C.* and *A.D.* Then I asked
the class, "What's so special about Jesus
that we measure our time from the years
when he lived as a man on earth?"

During the thoughtful pause that
followed, sixteen pairs of dark eyes looked
inquiringly at me and then at one another.
Finally, one boy spoke. He formed his
answer as a question: "No more lambs killed?"

The Navajo people are shepherds. All
of the youths in my class had early
recollections of tending sheep and goats with

their mothers and older brothers and sisters. The death of a lamb held deep meaning for them, and this young boy had beheld the Lamb of God from his shepherd's perspective.

No more lambs killed. Jesus is *the* Lamb. To behold him and his mercy is to see universality and intimacy at once. It is to see the red trail of thousands of sheep and goats slain in sacrifice, with no power to atone, leading up to the Cross—the saving event.

Jesus was the last lamb; there will be no more sacrifices, *no more lambs killed.* I am grateful for that shepherd's eye as I seek anew to *behold the Lamb of God.*

Remembering Jesus

Remember Jesus Christ, risen from the dead . . .
                                    2 Timothy 2:8

To behold the Lamb of God is to remember Jesus. It is to move by faith beyond the atoning death to the victory of the resurrection.

As faith becomes memory and expectation, Jesus lives on in us. When he said, "Do this in remembrance of me," he left no depth of Christian experience untouched. But what does it mean to remember? Does it mean that we should let the facts of the New Testament, the Good News, rest lightly on our consciousnesses? That we should be ready for God-talk at a moment's notice? That we should keep up an endless and repetitive conversation about religion?

True remembering is none of these. When we deceive ourselves into thinking that remembering means reciting or lecturing, we lose sight of the fact that remembering really means *receiving*. When we remember Jesus, we are shaped and sustained, nourished and formed by him. We feed our expectations on our faith in him. We grow because of God's gracious activity within us. We sense a bigger and bigger God, and are able to accept and respond to him, to trust him more and more.

Remembering is more than an intellectual experience; it is a *total response*. When we as Christians remember Jesus together, we share each others' gifts. By defining ourselves in terms of our common expectations and memories, we reinforce the fact that we belong to the same family and are of the same body: the body of Christ, risen from the dead.

Living Compassion

When he saw the crowds, he had compassion for them . . . .

Matthew 9:36

"People are so mean these days," the gas station attendant said to me.

"Why do you say that?" I asked.

"Just because," he answered. "They think it's all my fault. You know — the price of gasoline."

I drove away in a reflective mood. His words reminded me of a scene in a grocery store a few days before. I had stopped in to pick up a few small items, including tea. So there I was, prowling through the supermarket, when at last I found the tea shelf. But I also found something I wasn't expecting — a frozen chicken! Behold, a chicken with the tea!

Finding it still rock-hard, I returned it to its proper place and said to the poultry man, "I can't understand how anybody could do a thing like this."

"Oh, it happens all the time," he said, barely looking up from his work.

What needless trouble we cause for each other! A little consideration and a few kind words go a long way. Jesus' life serves as an example: *When he saw the crowds, he had compassion for them, because they were harassed and helpless, like sheep without a shepherd.*

We're all harassed by day-to-day living. We're all helpless in the face of things we can't understand, wrongs we can't correct, events we can do nothing about. How much better off the world would be if we all had more compassion, and could better understand the dark and difficult moods of ourselves and others.

Each of us needs practice in walking in someone else's shoes, in seeing things from another perspective. We need to learn to condemn less and understand more, to reject less and accept more.

Jesus, our Shepherd, walks among us this day. He views each one of us singly. Rather than seeing us as objects for ridicule or exploitation, he welcomes us as his sisters and brothers to be treasured and served, to be received with compassion.

Chapter Four:

Receiving the Answer

Ask, and it will be given you; seek, and you will find; knock, and it will be opened to you.

Matthew 7:7

I Thank You, Lord

Thank you, Lord,
for always answering prayer,
but not indulging
my every petty, private *give me*.
Thank you for winnowing and refining,
vetoing and delaying,
refusing and revising.

Thank you for being God
and never less,
for freeing me for wide horizons,
for protecting me from
my limited vision
and wayward will.

Thank you for foiling my every effort
to unseat you
and make myself king.
Thank you for keeping it safe
for me to pray.

Asking with Thanksgiving

Have no anxiety about anything, but in everything by prayer and supplication with thanksgiving let your requests be made known to God.

Philippians 4:6

How many times have we all wondered, "Is it wrong of me to ask God for specific things? Should I keep going to him with personal requests and petitions? Does he really want to be bothered with my day-to-day wants and needs?"

Rather than worrying about how we should and shouldn't pray — and what we should and shouldn't pray for — we might ask ourselves, "Where else would he want us go go?" Our Father loves to hear from us. He wants to know both our large and small requests. The large ones voice our boldness and confidence as we approach him; the small ones express our intimacy with him. He never refuses or forgets to answer a prayer. He never rejects any one of us; he always listens.

How do we know this? How can we be sure? Aren't our hands and hearts sometimes empty after we've finished praying? What about those times when we pray and seem to hear nothing but silence in return?

We know, we can be sure, that God hears and answers us because we know and can be sure that he loves us. He may grant the request, or he may give us something better, or he may remove our desire. He may fill us with the strength to endure, or he may wait to answer us fully and finally in heaven.

As we're wondering about these things, it's important to remember to pray *with thanksgiving.* Only when we go to our Father thankfully do we let our faith run ahead of our prayers and honor him with childlike trust. When we approach him with joy and gratitude for the great gifts he's already given us, and the love he's already shown us, we can be sure that he will welcome what we have to say *this day.*

Our Lord Answers:
By Granting the Request

A pastor in a rugged Norwegian seaport was in a whimsical mood. "It seems that most of my congregation must have been lost at sea," he mused.

When his listener was puzzled, the pastor explained. "More than half of the members have at one time or another asked that I pray for their safe journey. But hardly ten have returned to ask that I offer thanks."

Sometimes God isn't subtle. He simply gives us what we want. We pray for a safe journey, and we return home unharmed. We pray for the return of good health, and we experience it. We pray for success in a particular venture, or for the healing of some emotional wounds, and our prayers are answered. These are all *Thank God* moments. We all know them. The grace chapters go on and on as our Father writes them in his legible hand.

But how often do we think or thank? How often do we stop to voice our gratitude or to offer love in return for loving care? We get lost in the business of daily living and let ourselves rush past the meaning of life.

Gift-giving nourishes a relationship and helps it grow. Thanklessness blights both giving and receiving, and thoughtlessness hinders the course of love. When we give a gift to someone we love, we expect to be thanked. If the person forgets to thank us, we're hurt. When we forget to thank a loved one for a gift we've received, we chastise ourselves. How can we treat our heavenly Father with any less consideration than we expect from one another? *In everything . . . with thanksgiving.*

Our Lord Answers:
By Giving Something Better

Sometimes we pray, and then don't recognize God's answer when it comes. We ask for a certain thing, or event, or solution to a problem, and when God's response doesn't conform to our specifications we feel as if he hasn't heard us.

How shortsighted we can be! We need to distance ourselves from our own *I Wants* before we can see that our Father's way is the only good. Because we're so close to the present moment and can't see above or beyond it, we let ourselves despair and shed mistaken tears.

Picture the child who weeps into his pillow because he asked for a new tricycle and was answered with a *no*. Angry and withdrawn, he feels as if his parents have cut him off from their love. What he doesn't know is that father and mother have talked it over and have a plan. There will be a new bicycle next month, for his birthday — a gift for one who will soon outgrow his immediate wishes. His loving parents are thinking bigger thoughts than he is, and are running ahead of their child to do even more for him than he asked.

God, in his wisdom and love, is often running ahead of our wishes and prayers. He knows that we'll outgrow our present dreams, and he's already making plans to fulfill our future ones. His counsel is a gentle *wait and see*.

Sometimes, God's providence must be read backward. Then we can thank him for the gifts we never expected and couldn't recognize at the time. Our Father rescues us from our limited imaginations. He does far more for us than all we could ever begin to ask or think. He's able—and willing—to give us the kingdom.

Our Lord Answers: By Removing the Desire

Who among us hasn't at some time passionately pursued a mistaken goal or fallen in love with a potential disaster? A person, a dream, a position—anything may seem at the moment to be the pearl of pearls.

From a distance, we smile at these unrealized dreams. Once the fever has left us, we're able to see clearly what we were spared. We admit to our "good fortune" and go on with the business of living.

What happened to our earlier prayers —and why and how did it happen? We only know that we outgrew the need for what seemed so essential at the time. We set our sights on higher goals, and forgot the lesser ones. Our urgencies shifted. New excitements crowded out the old.

We never grow up to — much less outgrow — the privilege and promise of Christian prayer, but we *do* outgrow many of the prayers themselves. God mercifully guides us through the years, by leading us quietly or calling us dramatically to follow him. And following him almost always involves leaving something else behind — a dream, a goal, a wish. They left all, scripture tells us — home towns, people, property, fish nets, tax booths, water pots — and followed him. So the story goes. Living means leaving for the purpose of arriving at a new place; among the things we leave behind are some of our prayers.

At times, the Spirit leads us so gently that we can't even tell when we've abandoned a particular prayer. We're so caught up in the moment that we don't even notice. We don't look back or say goodbye. The step that takes us away draws us ever forward.

Even now, we can be sure that our Father has greater plans for us than we can bear to know or see. Glory — blinding, blazing, awesome glory — awaits each of us, and it's more of a miracle than we can handle at this time and in this place.

Our Lord Answers: By Giving Strength to Endure

God has a dream. That dream is you. He loves you as you are, but he loves you far too much to let you remain as you are. You yourself know that you can be so much more.

Sometimes, when I tell myself that God has a dream for me, I find myself resisting. I have a counter-dream. I want to be left alone. "Get out of my life!" I want to say, but the Lord is too wise and kind to let me settle into what I am. He knows what I'm capable of.

Sometimes I ask God to strengthen my faith and am surprised when he gives me a heavier load. I need to remind myself that faith doesn't grow in darkness and shelter.

The oak must be tested in the wind—and it must stand alone.

The great preacher Phillips Brooks once challenged his people to "Pray not for light burdens, but for strong backs!" Sometimes, I'd rather avoid a test than try my best to pass it. I need to remember that just as an arm grows strong when it lifts heavier and heavier weights, so also is faith exercised by difficulties and trying times. How can we be sure of our faith until we're led into the moment of truth and asked to live out what we sometimes too easily confess and affirm?

We gain great peace when we learn to accept our pain. Suffering is God's servant when it's placed in his free hand. Some of the choicest joys are ours when we obey his command to *wait and see*.

When we feel that our prayers aren't being answered, we mustn't let ourselves think that God is a disapproving parent who is punishing us. Rather, we aren't grown-up yet, and he's helping us to grow. His grown-up children are in heaven, at his side. Heaven is God's dream for us fulfilled.

Our Lord Answers:
Fully and Finally in Heaven

*. . . and God will wipe away every tear from
their eyes.*

Revelation 7:17

I was a thousand miles from home,
a visitor at a morning worship
service. This one, I found, offered more than
the liturgy, sermon, hymns, and handshakes.

The church custodian was leaving
after having served well and long. The
congregation was taking time this morning to
honor him. They called him forward to give
him gifts and offer him spoken tributes.
They talked of how he had never rebuffed
even the shyest child, of how he had labored
with patience and humor regardless of the
situation. One description of him stays in my
memory: "He never lost sight of the large
picture."

The large picture. Can we see it, you
and I? God has made room for each of us in
a picture which is too immense, too
profound for time or space to encompass. He
gives us a glimpse of it: "Who are these,

clothed in white robes, and whence have they come? . . . These are they who have come out of the great tribulation; they have washed their robes and made them white in the blood of the Lamb. Therefore are they before the throne of God, and serve him day and night within his temple; and he who sits upon the throne will shelter them with his presence. They shall hunger no more, neither thirst any more; the sun shall not strike them, nor any scorching heat. For the Lamb in the midst of the throne will be their shepherd, and he will guide them to springs of living water; and God will wipe away every tear from their eyes."

What a wonderful vision this is! Our Father, through his grace, lets us see beyond our present incompleteness and emptiness to his bountiful fullness. He helps us to look further than the ache of the present to the beauty of his endless future. There is a room waiting in his house for each of us.

We can't measure the success of our prayers by immediate results, or even by the results we have to look backward to see.

Instead, we can take comfort in knowing that God has saved a place for each of his children in heaven. That's the *large picture* in the family album.

Chapter Five:

Welcoming
the Child Within Us

*Truly, I say to you, unless you turn and
become like children, you will never enter the
kingdom of heaven.*

Matthew 18:3

To a Child

O, little one,
O, helpless one,
O, great receiver,
teach me.

Teach me
to be at home with gift,
to be at peace with need,
to rejoice in my belonging.

Teach me
to trust beyond all seeing,
to be blessed beyond all knowing,
to rest in God's pure Being.

Our Shepherd

I t was a concert in the park, and
my friend and her little granddaughter
were enjoying it together.   The child
was completely captivated by this, her first
orchestra concert. She sat transfixed
through each number, and then, forgetful of
her surroundings, she moved a bit closer
each time the music stopped. With Grandma
following each time she moved, at last she
was as close as she could get. She stood at
the very foot of the stage, lost in the sights
and sounds of the many instruments.

The concert ended, and for a brief,
anxious moment the child realized how far
she'd wandered. Then she turned to see her
grandmother standing behind her. With a
smile of relief, she cried, "Oh, I knew that I
could depend on you, Grandma!"

It's good to be sought after when we
stray. It's great to be cared for when we
forget. How fortunate we are that the Good
Shepherd follows us more faithfully than we
follow him. Like sheep, we nibble ourselves
lost, wandering in trivia and minor
distractions. Or we run our panic-stricken

way into the wilderness because faith fails us and our fears take over.

God never leaves us alone, not even for a moment. He never allows us to lose ourselves, no matter how hard we try. Even when we feel most isolated, we are never forsaken. God's silences don't signal abandonment. He is always with us.

It isn't flattering to be likened to sheep; the one thing they do well is bleat. But their bleating, as simple as it is, is their call for help. It's humbling to cry out our dependence, but it is wonderful to be able to say, "Father, I knew I could depend on you!"

Seeing Him

. . . for he endured as seeing him who is invisible.
Hebrews 11:27

I am encouraged by something that happened just yesterday. We were waiting for dinner, enjoying a relaxing conversation as adults, but listening to a six-year-old's running commentary on the subject of dinosaurs. He was drawing a picture for us as he talked of meat-eaters, plant-eaters, and other interesting details he'd learned at school. All the while, he continued drawing his picture.

When he had finished, he showed it to each of us in turn. We all praised the picture with its two dinosaurs against a detailed scenic background. The young artist received our compliments with dignity and pleasure, and then said calmly, "And there's a lake that doesn't show."

A lake that doesn't show. The child has eyes for the invisible! He lives in his unfettered imagination and frolics there. He makes happy use of a gift that most of us have shelved as unworthy of adult behavior.

Imagination is more than a playground for the mind; it's the banquet table of the heart, and a vital source of strength and energy for our daily struggles. Moses endured *as seeing him who is invisible.* He had a vision of God, and he drew strength from that vision. This great man welcomed the child who lived within him.

There's a child within each of us, regardless of our age, and this part of ourselves must not be denied. For it is this child who rises up expectantly to follow, who trusts the Father's promise, who sits in Jesus' lap and knows the peace and comfort there.

I'm So Glad

A friend was planning a vacation for his family of six — a rather ambitious holiday to various points in Europe. As departure time drew near, he spent many hours with maps, itineraries, and other travel information spread out on a large table in front of him.

A few days before they were due to begin their journey, the youngest of his children came into the room where her father was working. She peered over his shoulder at the maps and papers. She watched for a while as he went from one stack of papers to another, taking notes and adding to the growing list he was making. Finally, she climbed up in his lap and said contentedly, "Oh, I'm so glad all I have to do is just go along!"

This is the mark of a trusting child: the willingness to feel secure in another's hands. And this is the mark of the children of God: a willingness to welcome the unknown future and commit themselves to the Father's hands.

If you saw three small children seated in the family station wagon, dressed and ready for a vacation, would you ask them, "Where are you going? Which highway will you take? Where will you sleep tonight?" They probably wouldn't know, and such questions would only distress them. A better question might be, "Who are you going with?" Then they would answer, "With Mom and Dad!" They would speak dear names and affirm their love and trust.

Every day of our lives, we make choices, judgments, and decisions. We have the opportunity to exercise whatever talents we've been given. Beyond the areas we can control, however, lies the vast domain of our helplessness; it is when we enter this domain that we must be willing to admit our total dependence on our Father. Then we too can celebrate the fact that we are in God's hands, and that we can *just go along,* knowing that he'll bring us to the right destination.

Going to the Father

Yesterday as I walked down the airport ramp to board a plane, a family of four was in front of me, mother carrying the younger child and father holding the other by the hand. The older girl appeared to be about four and her every step was a bounce. She radiated expectancy and joy. It was obvious that this was *the day,* the day that had been talked about and planned for. She couldn't wait!

Her father looked down at her and asked, "Where are we going?"

"To Grandma's!" she shouted, punctuating her words with a higher bounce than usual.

She didn't say "to Bismarck" or "Billings," but "to Grandma's." As far as she was concerned, she was going to a person — the place didn't matter. She was an eloquent witness to the fact that we home in those who love us, in people more than in places.

Where are we going when we die? Everyone has the right to ask, but perhaps it's the wrong question. Rather, we should wonder, *To whom am I going?* Again and again during his lifetime on earth, our Lord Christ said, "I go to my Father." To my father—to our Father.

How much more important this is than any speculation on what Heaven looks like.

We all want to unlock the deepest secrets of life and death. We need to remember, though, that Jesus holds the key. When we make his words our own, saying, "I go to my Father," we hold the key to the future — the only key we will ever need.

Always Special

There was a little boy whose class was preparing a dramatic presentation of the story of Peter Rabbit. He spoke of it nonstop to his family and friends, especially as the day drew near. Excitement ran high both at home and at school.

The day came—and along with it a big disappointment. The boy was sick and couldn't attend. His mother was especially sorry, and worried that his part would be missed. Finally, with one expansive gesture, the little actor said, "Don't worry Mom, the teacher's got two whole rows of us cabbages!"

Us cabbages. How well that describes us all at times. We each have days when we feel so ordinary, not special at all. But God's gift of mercy gives us worth even when we feel most unworthy. We live in the Father's forgiveness, and that makes us always special. No one whose life story is written in grace can be an ordinary person. And no day of grace is an ordinary day.

We can shake the cabbage-complex by turning away from ourselves and turning instead to face our trustworthy God. His abundant and active goodness singles each of us out. We are all his beloved children.

Sometimes, we may feel as if life is nothing more than a play, and that we're all just cabbages — insignificant, unworthy, expendable, replaceable. These are the times when we can look to our Father for comfort and reassurance. To the One who watches over us, all of us are special.

Chapter Six:

Welcoming All Things

We know that in everything God works for good with those who love him, who are called according to his purpose.

Romans 8:28

Lord, I Saw Two

I watched them today
on the merry-go-round,
waited for their smiles,
their waving hands,
each time around.

To others, one child
and one adult;
to me, two children.
No longer my grandchild
and her mother,
my daughter
and her daughter —
but two children,
riding the merry-go-round,
laughing.

One child,
but I saw two:
memory's trick photography
deepening joy and sorrow,
leaving me more exposed —
the price and pleasure
of the passing years.

Lord, I saw two:
for choicest wine left to the last
I thank you.

All Things Hold Together

We sat at a table in a Tokyo restaurant — a place of distinction with many wall hangings — when suddenly everything began to move. I watched, amazed, as the paintings near us swayed back and forth. After a few seconds, someone shouted, "Earthquake!"

It was my first. It lasted a very short while, caused no real damage, and wasn't a major event. Except for me. I had never lived through such a threat to myself and my surroundings, and I was profoundly impressed.

When we experience the shaking of what we have always thought to be unshakable, we are overwhelmed. We lose our bearings, and it seems as if there's nothing left to hold on to.

Although we may not be aware of it, perhaps all of us live in the fear of a spiritual earthquake. We're afraid that our world will fall apart. We have trouble believing that all things hold together in Christ, no matter what happens. Our God is one God, and in him rests the integrity and order of everything he has created.

"He is before all things, and in him all things hold together." During emotional upheavals and spiritual storms, we need to remember that "in everything God works for good with those who love him, who are called according to his purpose." We know that all things are not good; much that happens to us and around us is evil. Still, our Father is there with us. He takes evil and suffering to himself in the person of his Son, and through his grace turns it into good.

When Jesus said, "It is finished," the fight was over—but it was won, not lost. His last words before his death on earth proclaim his victory; we too are victors. Nothing can ever shake that fact.

Think About These Things

Finally, brethren, whatever is true, whatever is honorable, whatever is just, whatever is pure, whatever is lovely, whatever is gracious, if there is any excellence, if there is anything worthy of praise, think about these things.

Philippians 4:8

I have a friend who is admired by all who know him for his wisdom and creativity. Throughout his life he has been a voracious reader, but now his sight is failing.

Recently, he served as a resource person at a study workshop. After the workshop, I met a student who had attended, and asked, "Was he in his usual excellent form?"

"Yes," he answered, "I especially remember his opening remark. He was standing at the front of the room, looking out at us. We all knew that his eyesight was getting poorer. He waited for the room to become quiet, and said, 'I can't read much any more, so I don't think about as many things as I once did,' and then he paused and added, 'But I think more!' "

I think more. We seek breadth naturally. We frequently need no urging to be interested in many different things. We like to take pride in the fact that we're always learning something new. But when our options are suddenly narrowed through illness, or accident, or some other circumstance, we find ourselves with time we never had before. Although we wouldn't choose it, our sudden deprivation can be an act of grace. Without it, we might miss the chance to examine ourselves and reach new understanding. A crisis can help us stop, think, and absorb more fully the depths of God's will and purpose for us. This process can move us from being simply informed to being truly wise.

Paul the Apostle urges us to think selectively and with discrimination. He advises us to be less concerned about details, and to concentrate on what is *true, honorable, just, pure, gracious, excellent.* Our wisdom can flourish if we take the time to *think about these things.*

You Are Beautiful

I met a new friend only a few weeks ago. I communicate with her by writing large and legible words on a notepad she keeps at her side. Her sight and hearing are seriously impaired. After I write a message to her, she holds the notepad close to the light and reads the words aloud, slowly.

Recently, during an interesting exchange of spoken and written responses, she suddenly and painfully exclaimed, "If only I could read! I don't know *anything* any more. My children and grandchildren know so much more than I!" She let the notepad fall closed.

Hearing her distress, I took the pen and quickly wrote, "You are growing in wisdom every day, and you are beautiful."

She picked the pad up and read my words aloud: " . . . growing in wisdom every day and you are . . . ." Here she stopped, peered at me, and said with a smile, "Oh, you've been kissing the blarney stone!"

I quickly took the paper and wrote, "I mean it!"

Indeed, I did mean it — it wasn't

blarney at all. My friend is a sister in the faith who is seeking depth and finding it. And depth is beautiful, one of the rarest and choicest forms of human beauty.

People like her are called *shut ins*. Too often, we assume that because they can't move about, or read, or carry on conversations as freely as the rest of us, they're incapable of doing anything. We forget that at times like these the inward journey sometimes becomes easier. When our outer lives become limited, we are freer to let the Spirit explore the depths within us as he leads us to what is true.

So much human beauty lies hidden in the folds of the community of faith. Our Father calls us to seek it and to rejoice in it wherever it is found.

The Lord Needs Us All

Our need to be needed often causes us great anxiety. We hunger for the satisfaction of feeling that we are important to someone. We want to be recognized when we're present and missed when we're absent. Our egos need to be fed. But when we're in pursuit of this recognition, we sometimes settle for too little.

A young friend of mine was recently ordained into a ministry to students. When we met one day, and I asked him how his work was coming along, he said, "I believe I'm finally beginning to find my security in the gospel."

What a liberating answer that was! He wasn't looking for security from the students who gathered around him and asked for his guidance. Instead, he was looking to the gospel. Rather than seeking attention or applause, status or success, he was believing the Good News and sharing it with others. This is all the self-replenishing support any of us could ever need.

The Lord needs us to do his will. He asks his believers to let his Word become flesh in them. In their little incarnations, Christ's Incarnation can bear fruit. The Word dwells among us when it turns into hands and feet, hearts and heads — when it turns into you and me. Only then can the world behold its glory.

All of us are needed — the young to

keep the old youthful in heart and spirit; the old to share their wisdom and experience with the young. Each must help the other in the art of enjoying life's fruits while they are ripe. Youth tends to pluck the blossoms; age keeps the fruit until it's spoiled. The one won't wait, and the other won't let go.

When we come together to share our faith in Christ, we put ourselves in loving touch with God and one another. We're part of the Christian family. The Lord needs us all.

Following Our Lord

And he said to him, "Follow me."

Matthew 9:9

Whether you're eight or eighty, the call is still *Follow me.* Jesus calls us to a challenge continually new. To follow him is to participate, not just to observe; to get involved in new meanings and concerns, new experiences and responsibilities.

No one is ever "over the hill." That expression suggests that life is downhill the rest of the way. It implies that one's future is somehow in the past.

Some folks seem to confuse *retired* with *retarded*. They talk down, look down, think down to older people. They urge them to avoid challenge and confine themselves to busywork and hobbies for the rest of their lives. But when there's nothing to stretch us, we shrink. When our initiative and courage aren't tested, we grow flabby and fearful. When we start thinking less of ourselves, we become less than ourselves.

Recreation is fine, but it's not a career, nor does it give life enough meaning. It can lead to an artificial and trivial existence and make retirement the hardest work of all. No one has ever "had it" when it comes to doing good or leading a worthwhile life.

The Lord is always on the move. In order to keep up with him, we need to keep our spirits active and be willing to move beyond the known into the unknown and untried. We must reach deep within ourselves to find the trusting child who still lives there, the one who isn't afraid to take risks.

The call is still *Follow me;* the speaker is the ever-contemporary Jesus.

Learning to Be Content

I have learned, in whatever state I am, to be content.

Philippians 4:11

She has much reason to complain. Her physical senses are badly impaired. And yet, I'm always blessed when I visit with her. So I said, "It's nice to be with you."

"Oh, you are kind," she answered, "but there are days when I hate myself because I'm such a complainer!"

Such a complainer. As she said the words, I could almost hear a camera click, for I know I'm in the picture. Sometimes when I suffer disappointments or sickness, dark moods come. I turn in on myself and can't get my own weight off my hands. I know it's my fault and I feel guilty that I'm doing it, but the more I concentrate on myself, the darker I get. I can't separate myself from my depression.

It is a common condition. Self-hatred is like a weed threatening our growth, overwhelming us until we can no longer move, or give, or even feel the warmth of God's love. But we are never hidden from God; his care and protection will clear away the weeds until we see that we still have much to give. We can grow again, nourished by the constant renewal of the Holy Spirit in our hearts.

The veteran Apostle Paul proclaims this source of strength. *I have learned,* he writes, *in whatever state I am, to be content . . . I can do all things in him who strengthens me.* He looks through the circumstance at Christ. He regains and sustains perspective by thinking less of what happens *to* him and more of what happens *in* him. He believes his present state is transient and his place with God is permanent.

Dag Hammarskjold has some strong words for himself and for us when we start to close ourselves off: "Give me something to die for — ! What makes loneliness and anguish is not that I have no one to share my burden, but this: I have only my burden to bear."

These words caution us about the dangers of worrying too much about ourselves. When our focus is on others, we find less reason to complain. When we bear a burden other than our own, then we can learn to be content.

Looking to Jesus

. . . let us run with perseverance the race that is set before us, looking to Jesus the pioneer and perfecter of our faith, who for the joy that was set before him endured the cross, despising the shame, and is seated at the right hand of the throne of God.

Hebrews 12:1-2

Our Father sent his son Jesus
to live in the world as a man,
and nothing was ever the same again.
Jesus turned things around. Because of
his victory over death, the future is no
longer controlled by the past. The past
is controlled by the future. Because
our sins are fully forgiven, the burden
of all our yesterdays has fallen off.
Looking to Jesus, we can forget what
needs to be forgotten. We can be
forever free.

Jesus pioneered our salvation, and so
we too embrace the same pioneer spirit. We
live in expectation, not regret, looking
forward and upward in our life and service.
Because of Jesus, we live our lives in the
morning light of hope and love.

A contemporary writer once described her aging father in this way: "He never left the prow of the boat, where he could feel the spray of the future on his face."

For the joy that was set before him, Jesus endured the cross. The same joy awaits us. Sometimes, when we're especially depressed or feel as if our life is coming to an end, we can remind ourselves of this fact. The most difficult challenge we face is the call to stay truly alive until we die, to live in the prow and feel the spray, to continue to expect great things of our Father and ourselves.

Keeping the Faith

The time of my departure has come. I have fought the good fight, I have finished the race, I have kept the faith. Henceforth there is laid up for me the crown of righteousness, which the Lord, the righteous judge, will award me on that Day, and not only to me but also to all who have loved his appearing.

2 Timothy 4:6b-8

In these words Paul says to Timothy, "It's worth it!" The foot-blistering, lung-stretching race is over. The finish line has been reached, and the old man is saying to the younger, "Keep on the track! All your training and struggling will be amply rewarded. Don't be a quitter!"

Paul struggled throughout his life—not *in order that* he could belong to Christ, but *because* he did belong to him. The good fight is defined by the life of faith. And this is the life of one who has received the family name in baptism, not one who is trying to earn it by winning special honors.

Paul lived as one who belonged. He never claimed that everything was easy because he belonged with Jesus Christ, but he did emphasize that the pains and sorrows, the struggles and seeming losses all had meaning. They all led up to the "finish line." They resulted in something significant and good.

Henceforth there is laid up for me the crown of righteousness. Paul had something to look forward to—his Father's guarantee. We have the same Father and can expect the same rewards. Paul's words to Timothy are full of meaning for us today: old and young alike can begin, continue, and complete their ministry in this same hope.

Learning to Comfort

Blessed be the God and Father of our Lord Jesus Christ, the Father of mercies and God of all comfort, who comforts us in all our affliction, so that we may be able to comfort those who are in any affliction, with the comfort with which we ourselves are comforted by God.

2 Corinthians 1:3-4

Many years ago a great teacher, Joseph Parker, told his students: "There is nothing which a man in grief dreads so much as uncomforting comfort; he cannot bear to be spoken to by those who do not know what comfort really is."

True comfort gives us strength to go on, and there are times when we all need it. Comfort comes to us as we embrace and then resolve and put aside our suffering. There is no comfort in denial and escape.

102

Saying "I musn't feel this way," brings us no resolution. True comfort allows us to own our feelings and then to turn away from our pain to the God of all comfort.

Comfort comes through faith-sharing, through turning together to Christ. It is one beggar showing another where there is food, the healed one gossiping about the skill of a physician, the at-home one inviting the homeless to share a home together. It is passing on the good which we receive and allowing it to multiply by sharing.

When We're Weak

Sometimes she seems to look past me. She makes me feel that she's smiling at God. A visit with her brings me a new awareness of God's care and goodness. At the end of our last visit, I rose to leave saying, "You've given me much today."

"Oh, no, I'm too weak for that!" was her reply.

"But that's probably the reason you're able to help," I said.

Perhaps it is her very weakness that helps to heal me. She dramatizes my dependence on God. She turns me back to the source of my being.

The tired and tested Apostle Paul lived in the Lord's promise: "My grace is sufficient for you, for my power is made perfect in weakness." Paul responded with this pledge: "I will all the more gladly boast of my weaknesses, that the power of Christ may rest upon me . . . for when I am weak, then I am strong."

The bearing walls of a building are mostly hidden. But they are its strength. Perhaps it is so with the human community. Much of its strength remains hidden in those who pray and reflect and endure, in those who say, when reminded of the parts they play, "Oh, I am too weak for that!"

God's power is at work wherever our weakness invites his presence.

Keeping Faith Active

"It is in the nature of faith to study."
My friend said this in a casual
conversation, and he is a wise man. The
statement made me wonder. Doesn't true
faith consist of acceptance without question?
Or do we sometimes forget that in order to
find, we must first be willing to seek?

Faith is "the assurance of things
hoped for, the conviction of things not
seen." If this is so, then why study? Faith is
trusting, resting, following, sometimes
waiting—all while relying on our Lord Jesus
Christ. This faith is our foundation, the
roots of the tree.

But what about the trunk and the
branches? What is faith when it breaks
above ground for everyone to see, when it's
not passive, but active?

It is love. And love wants to know.
Love inquires. It asks and asks again, it
waits patiently for answers. It presses and
probes, exploring the heart's reasons behind
the reasons of the mind.

Love is never satisfied. Notice how
people in love behave: they observe each

other's every word and gesture, they explore each implication and attitude. Love's favorite language is the question. Love reads. Love listens. Attention is its first gift. "Faith active in love," scripture calls it. My friend was right. Faith must be active in order to grow, to move, to stay alive.

The Magic Moment

I was in the Palmer House in Chicago — one of fifteen hundred teachers attending a convention. It was the Wednesday evening before Thanksgiving Day, and time for the closing celebration. As we entered the auditorium, we were given surprising instructions: "Don't forget to pick up your potato."

And there they were, piled along the back wall in that elegant auditorium, bushels and bushels of potatoes! We did as we'd been told, and then received another surprising instruction: "And now we'll give you exactly two minutes of silence with your potato."

Silence in the auditorium. We sat, wondering what to do next. Then I began to think, touch, feel, smell. I remembered things I'd learned about the potato long ago and since almost forgotten. Cut it skillfully, making sure there's an eye on each piece, and you'll have as many new plants as there are pieces. The green spot is where the sun has scorched it — it leaves a bitter taste. This rough spot is where it will begin to decay.

That plain, brown potato took on new life and new meaning in my hand. I thought of how many millions of people this simple root has kept alive in good times and bad.

Those two minutes reminded me that common experiences often introduce us to the uncommon. We owe a debt of awe and wonder to one another and to every living thing on earth. When we're able to sense the uniqueness of each passing moment, even the most ordinary of events can carry deep meaning.

The ceremony in the Palmer House changed me, making me more sensitive to gifts, more ready to give thanks. Any growing thing might have been used to achieve the same purpose — an acorn, a string bean, a strawberry. Every living thing praises the God of life simply by the fact of its existence.

What do you see around you? The sun shining, a green leaf uncurling on a branch, a squirrel foraging for its dinner? All things, no matter how small or common, can offer glimpses of our oneness with God and his creation.

Active Love

Today I was arrested as I drove in city traffic. No, I wasn't stopped by an officer and I didn't pay a fine, but I was arrested nevertheless.

It was the evening rush hour, and I was alone. I had absentmindedly left the radio on, and I wasn't really listening to it when the summons came: "If you were arrested for being a Christian, would there be enough evidence to convict you?"

I had to answer even if there was nobody there, "Who, me? What do you mean—evidence? Do you mean love?"

I had answered my own question. God's love is a verb, and he, through *his* love, has acted to rescue me. Sometimes, I try to make God's love a noun; this permits me to keep him at a distance, to postpone or avoid action. This active love is evidence of our Christianity.

Jesus warns us not to turn love into a noun when he asks us to understand that he lives in everyone we meet: "I was hungry," he says, "and you gave me no food, I was thirsty and you gave me no drink, I was a stranger and you did not welcome me, naked and you did not clothe me, sick and in prison and you did not visit me. . . . Truly, I say to you, as you did it not to one of the least of these, you did it not to me."

Martin Luther has described the active commitment our love must make: "Faith, like light, should always be simple and unbending, while love, like warmth, should beam forth on every side and bend to every necessity of the brethren."

When the day of my final "arrest" comes, I pray that there will be enough evidence to convict me.

Chapter Seven:

Child of God, Come Home

Now to him who by the power at work within us is able to do far more abundantly than all that we ask or think, to him be glory in the church and in Christ Jesus to all generations, for ever and ever. Amen.

Ephesians 3:20-21

Is It So?

I heard it said just yesterday
by one who ought to know
that struggling vines
yield choicest wine;
hardworking, fighting vines,
reaching, clinging, stretching
past stubborn rocks
to distant water —
just enough
to stay alive.

Is it always so,
true of growing things
like you and me?
Must sweetest wines
from the human vine
come through grief and struggle?

With grace of sun and soil and wind,
life is born of testing.
Our spirits reach past granite burdens
through painful loss
to greater gain.

Come Home to Give Thanks

A child, new in the neighborhood and accustomed to praying at mealtime, was a dinner guest in a neighbor's home. When everyone began to eat, he brightly asked in surprise, "Don't you pray before you eat?" When the answer was "no," he said, intending no offense, "Oh, you're just like my dog, you start right in!"

Why *do* we pray? Is it simply because we are creatures of God? No, that can't be the whole answer, for every living thing is God's creature, too. The whole answer is this: We are creatures in his image. We are meant for prayer and praise. We can never fully realize how close we are to our Father until we learn to live in daily thanksgiving and take the time to celebrate the source of our being.

Life takes on meaning and purpose when we add to it the deepening power of prayer. Praise is the most fitting of all human activities. Rather than hindering our work in the world, it enhances it. Rather than destroying or hampering our pleasure, it sanctifies it.

We have all heard small boys bragging about their fathers; in this way they show their love and confidence. Our prayers and thanksgiving are evidence of our love and confidence in God, our Father.

I have heard it said that the saddest moment for the unbeliever is when he is truly thankful and has no one to thank. To receive the gift and to cut oneself off from the Giver is to live in loneliness and incompleteness. God offers himself to each of us. We belong to his family. Let us give thanks!

Come Home to Rest

I cherish what my sister has told me about her problem.

One evening at bedtime she went to our father and asked, "May I talk with you? I have a problem."

"Of course. What is it?" he answered.

Then it came: "I almost always fall asleep while I'm praying my prayers."

His reply was immediate: "Well, is there a better way to fall asleep?"

I like to think of this story. It tells me much about my father, and even more about my Father, God. Surely, my father's advice to my sister didn't mean that we should wait for fatigue to overtake our prayers and let that suffice for our relationship with God. Instead, it meant that since sleep is the ultimate act of trust, God's child is no less his child when he or she falls asleep while talking with him.

Sleep leaves us helpless, defenseless. It comes only when we're at peace with our surroundings or are so weary that we can't stay awake. As we relax and find release from our cares, we respond to the invitation to rest in the Lord. Our Father is honored when we home in him. Is there any better shelter for sleep than prayer?

When you need to replenish your strength and revive your courage, rest on the faithfulness and power of God. Let the arms of his mercy hold you. Relieve your aching self through full confession to him. Luxuriate under the warm covers of his forgiveness. Pillow your head on affirmation. And if you fall asleep while praying, leave *Amen* to God.

Come Home to Grow

But grow in the grace and knowledge
of our Lord and Savior Jesus Christ.
To him be the glory both now
and to the day of eternity. Amen.

2 Peter 3:18

Well I remember the pencil marks
on the door casing between the
kitchen and living room in my childhood
home. Each mark signified the growing of
a child.

I had grown rapidly and was tall for
my age. I loved to read my initials and look
down at the lowest marks. "Was I ever as
short as that?" I'd ask. I was proud.

But there is no pride in growing in
grace. The spotlight isn't on me, but on
God. Not "Am I taller, kinder, more
honest, more patient, more courageous?"
No, the light swings away and turns on him.
To him be glory both now and to the day of eternity.
Is my God bigger today than he was a year
ago, five years ago, or ten? Do I trust him
more? Do I leave more to him? Am I less
tied up in myself?

117

Grace. What is it but God's loving activity in my life? To grow in grace is to see more and more clearly the moving finger of the One who writes the story of my life. I praise God when I forget myself. And I grow in grace.

Come Home to Forgive

. . . one thing I do, forgetting what lies behind and straining forward to what lies ahead, I press on toward the goal for the prize of the upward call of God in Christ Jesus.

Philippians 3:13-14

The truly Christian memory is adept at forgetting what needs to be forgotten and remembering what needs to be remembered. It can sort through the remembrances of a lifetime, tossing out the bad, saving the good. It can discriminate.

We sometimes regret our inability to remember, but we often ignore our failure to forget. We lose sight of the fact that Christ has made us his own. Because of him, our goal is not to collect all the data of our lifetimes, but, as Paul puts it, to concentrate on "the surpassing worth of knowing Christ Jesus my Lord."

When we fail to forgive, we retain memories which become intolerable baggage on the inward journey. When we cling to resentments and jealousies, we cripple ourselves with increasing bitterness. Whenever we refuse to let go of the trivial, we sap our strength for shouldering what's essential.

As we grow in age and in grace, we should remember that persons suffer more depression and despair because they can't forgive and forget than because they can't remember.

Forgiveness is a beautiful form of forgetfulness. This Christian absentmindness is truly heaven-sent.

Come Home to Hear the Story

*One generation shall laud thy works to another,
and shall declare thy mighty acts.*

Psalm 145:4

A friend recently returned from a three-month stay in Central Africa, where he served as a consultant in a translating and teaching program. One evening, we gathered to hear him speak of his experiences there.

As he took his nightly jeep ride through the bush, he told us, he could see the village fires shining through the darkness. Around each fire, he knew, were young and old people who had come to hear the old men tell "the story." What they were listening to was the story of their tribe. This continual storytelling was their way of sharing their heritage, a way of making sure it passed from one generation to the next.

We nourish each other whenever we gather to tell and retell the story as we find it in the scriptures and experience it in the daily goodness of God. We help and shape one another when we come together in the common circle around the fire of God's love.

Too often in our Christian witness, we have depended on argument to get our point across. We turn the church into a debating society and let ourselves become too preoccupied with proofs. We forget resistance thrives in an adversary situation; there are always a thousand defenses against our arguments, no matter how forceful we are. But who can resist the warmth and power of the story well told? *One generation shall laud thy works to another. . . .*

The human family strengthens as its members permit their personal histories to be woven into the tapestry of one great story. We add to it every day as we experience God's presence, receive his gifts, and pass on what we have learned to one another.

God offers himself to us; we, in turn, share what we receive from him. This is the meaning of the Christian story. In a graceful cycle of faith, we move from God to each other and back to God again. Our movement is both personal and communal. It binds together the past and future, and through it we come together in the presence of the Father, the Son, and the Spirit.

References

The following lists the sources of quoted material that are not indicated in the text itself.

Introduction, Psalm 90:1-2
I'm Not Lost, John 1:1
A Family Prayer, Luke 11:1 and 8:21
God Is for Me, Romans 8:31-32
A Child of Light, John 10:10 and Matthew 4:4
Our Lord Answers: Fully and Finally in Heaven,
    Revelation 7:13-17
All Things Hold Together, Colossians 1:17 and Romans 8:28
Learning to Be Content, *Markings* (Knopf, 1964) p. 85
When We're Weak, 2 Corinthians 12:9-10
Keeping Faith Active, Hebrews 11:1
Active Love, Matthew 25:42,43,45
Come Home to Forgive, Philippians 3:8

Alphabetical Index